Violence in Television Fiction

David Docherty

BROADCASTING STANDARDS COUNCIL

ANNUAL REVIEW 1990

PUBLIC OPINION AND BROADCASTING STANDARDS : 1

John Libbey
LONDON · PARIS · ROME

British Library Cataloguing in Publication Data
Docherty, David,
Violence in television fiction - (Public opinion and broadcasting standards)
1.Television programmes. Violence
I. Title II Series
302.2345

ISBN: 0-86196 284 2
ISSN: 0960-3999

Published by
John Libbey & Company Ltd.,
13 Smiths Yard, Summerley St, London SW18 4HR, UK. +44 (0)81 947 2777
John Libbey Eurotext Ltd.
6 rue Blanche, 92120 Montrouge, France. +33 (1) 47 35 85 52
John Libbey-CIC s.r.l.,
via L. Spallanzani 11, 00161 Rome, Italy. +39 (06) 873054/869810

Contents

Preface

From its inception in 1988, the Broadcasting Standards Council has laid particular emphasis on the importance of thorough research into public attitudes towards the broadcasting issues within its remit. This emphasis has been balanced by a developing programme of research into the possible effects of broadcasting on its audiences.

Under the first of these two headings, the Council published a general survey in its Annual Report for 1988 - 89. It now plans to undertake research annually into a specific area of its concerns and to give the findings separate publication. So, in 1990, we are publishing the results of a survey of public attitudes towards the portrayal of violence, this time in television fiction. The survey in 1991 will deal with matters of taste and decency. Then, in the last year of a three-year cycle, the concentration of interest will be on the portrayal of sex and sexuality. A number of the same questions will feature in each of the surveys in order to provide a continuity of view over such matters as the importance of the 9.00 p.m. television Watershed.

I and my colleagues hope that the outcome of these studies will enable us to make a continuing contribution to the general debate about broadcasting in times of change which seem likely to persist for the remainder of the century.

Lord Rees-Mogg

1.

Introduction

When we watch a violent scene in a television drama, do we see our vicious selves and malignant society staring back? Does television portray the world as a dangerous and chaotic place which can only be negotiated by brutal means or with fearful resignation; and then, on the next twist up in the interpretative spiral, does television show back to us the violence which the medium itself spawned? Or, is this all too gloomy? Is it closer to the truth that we see violent images as entertainment - merely as a bit of action to drive the story along? Are we robust viewers who regard television fiction as, by and large, an invention which has little bearing on our lives and attitudes?

It is easy to fall into two related but separate traps when reflecting on televised images of violence. The first hazard is the argument that television generates inconsequential symbols which glide along the surface of consciousness and are picked up or discarded like bric-a-brac in a cultural car boot sale; the second hazard is to regard images of fictional violence as if they were parasites which burrow deep into the consciousness and await time and circumstance to create havoc.

The only way to sustain these positions is either to reduce flesh and blood, argumentative people to empty-headed phantoms, or to regard every television programme as intellectual candy-floss. That it is impossible to sustain sweeping generalisations about the attitudes, values, and behaviour of television viewers will become apparent in this report.

The discussion which follows is based on two studies of public perception of violence **in television fiction** in Britain and one in Northern Ireland.[1]

The first project was a national survey of public opinion on violence in Britain and in British television fiction. The research company, Research International, interviewed one-thousand-and-nine people in Britain for the main survey. Research International also conducted specialist surveys of one-hundred-and-

---

1 *The Broadcasting Standards Council survey in 1989 focused in the main on violence in news and current affairs. Details can be found in the* **Broadcasting Standards Council Annual Report 1988-89**. *See also: Docherty, D. (1989) 'Handling the Horror Factor'.* **The Listener**, *2 November,; Docherty, D. (1990) 'A Death in the Home'.* **Sight and Sound**, *Spring.*

twelve people with access to Sky Television; fifty Asians and fifty Afro-Caribbeans; and, finally, in order to explore the distinctive experience of Northern Ireland, Research International interviewed one-hundred-and-fifty-seven people in the Province. (See appendix 1)

The second project focused on viewers in Northern Ireland; and it explored, in particular, their views about violence in drama. Fusion Research discussed these issues at four viewers' workshops, and it conducted in-depth interviews with two groups of teenagers and four families. (See appendix 2)

Finally, an experimental project was carried out by Network Research, who sent out video-tapes containing two dramas and a feature film to two-hundred-and-fifty viewers and invited them to act as if they were editing the material for transmission. (See appendix 3)

This account of these studies does not pretend to offer definitive answers to the Gordian-knotted questions about television and its effects[2]; it seeks, instead, to offer a reasonable number of clues about how viewers regard these matters, and to explore the reasons why many people in this country enjoy and are entertained by images of violence.

That there is public concern about violence on television has been established for many years. For example, Paul Croll, in a study for the BBC in the early 1970s, discovered a considerable fear among a majority of respondents (60%) in his survey that exposure to televised violence might trigger violent acts among unstable people. Moreover, many others (28%) worried that exposure to images of violence on television might make viewers insensitive to violent actions in real life[3]. Almost twenty years later, similar concerns were expressed in research conducted by the Independent Broadcasting Authority: most (78%) of the people who responded to the IBA's survey thought that 'People are justified in being concerned about the impact of TV violence on children today.'[4]

---

2 For accounts of psychological studies of violence on television see Cumberbatch G. and Howitt D. (1989) **A Measure of Uncertainty: The Effects of the Mass Media** (A Broadcasting Standards Council Monograph), John Libbey. Gunter, B. (1985) **Dimensions of Television Violence,** Gower Publishing. Kubey, R. Csikszentmihalyi, M. (1990) **Television and the Quality of LIfe,** How Viewing Shapes Everyday Experience, Lawrence Erlbaum Associates. For an alternative perspective on the subject see Davies, T. (1989) **The Man of Lawlessness: the media, violence and prophecy,** Hodder and Stoughton.
3 Croll, P. (1971) **The Nature of Public Concern with Television, with particular reference to violence,** BBC Broadcasting Research Department.
4 Gunter, B. Wober, M. (1988) **Violence on Television: What the Viewers Think,** John Libbey, (page 14). This report also showed that most respondents (64%) thought that children would imitate the violence which they see on television.

The Broadcasting Standards Council's exploration of public opinion about violence on television, conducted in 1990, shows that concerns about violence on television may result in a strong, emotional rejection of violent images. For example, as a result of being 'disgusted' by a programme, many people (24%) who replied to the questionnaire claimed that they had turned off their set, or walked out of the room, in the month before the survey took place. The reasons for this strong reaction varied; many of the responses (24%) were triggered by a violent image in a programme, whereas others were the result of swearing (19%), sex (25%), tasteless comedy (9%), politics (3%), or simply because the viewer thought that the programme was 'rubbish' (5%).[5]

Twenty years of research on public attitudes to violence on television suggests that concern about the portrayal of violent actions on the screen is related to deep worries about violence in society. George Gerbner, a US researcher who has spent much of his intellectual career exploring television violence, argued recently:

> What are some consequences of exposure to television's violent world? Studies have revealed that such exposure does occasionally incite viewers to violence and often desensitizes. But for most viewers, our studies have shown that television's mean and dangerous world cultivates a sense of relative insecurity, vulnerability, and mistrust, and - despite its supposedly 'entertaining' nature - alienation and gloom.[6]

Gerbner suggests strongly that a clear connection exists between watching television and attitudes to real-life violence. In order to assess the value of these insights for the study of television violence in the UK, the BSC survey explored attitudes to what many people think of as 'legitimate' violence - such as corporal and capital punishment. Moreover, the survey investigated respondents' fears about being physically attacked, and their general concerns about the level of violence in today's Britain.

Having established the nature and complexity of public response to punishment, crime and self-defence, this report relates these opinions to viewers' enjoyment of, or concern about, shootings, stabbings, beatings, car-chases, stage-coach-crashes, cartoon mayhem, pratfalls, close-calls, Shakespearean slaughter, and the rest of the inventive foul-play to which the catch-all term 'television violence' is attached. However, before one can understand the dramatic representation of violence, violent actions must be pinpointed culturally in the societies within which they are spawned, interpreted and justified.

---

5   Question: 'Have you turned the television off, changed channels, or walked out of the room in the last month because you personally were disgusted by an individual programme or scene within a TV programme?' N=total sample, 1009.

6   Gerbner, G. and Signorielli, N. (1990) **Violence Profile 1967 through 1988-89: Enduring Patterns**. Corporation for Public Broadcasting, Washington, Page 3.)

2.

Signs of Struggle

Struggles

There is a proverb which states glibly but disturbingly that 'every people loves its own form of violence.' If this proverb contains a vestige of insight, how do we come to love actions or the dramatic representation of actions which other cultures would regard as brutal, cruel or inhuman?

The **meaning** of violent acts varies according to the different contexts in which they take place. For example, the festival of violence - the crowds, the bustle, the pie-sellers, the high good humour - which often surrounded a public hanging, was acceptable in Britain before 1866, the last occasion on which it was carried out, but would seem barbarous to most people today. Indeed, the myriad ways of carrying out capital punishment are culturally specific: Spain garroted its murderers, France, the guillotine, the USSR shot people, the UK preferred hanging, states in the US ranged across the electric chair, lethal gas, shooting and injections.

Cultures which perceive themselves as violent, and which celebrate savage actions, can produce a disturbing indifference to human life. Auden's line that 'Terror like a frost shall halt the flood of thinking', was aimed at Nazi Germany - a society whose character was forged in brutality, but it can be applied easily to other late 20th Century cultures. Take, for example, the testimony of Lieutenant William Calley, who, as a US soldier, was responsible for the massacre of at least 109 men, women and children in a small Vietnamese village called My Lai. At his Court Martial, Calley was asked by his prosecutor, Aubrey Daniel, what his men were firing at in My Lai:

Calley: At the enemy, sir.

Daniel: At people?

Calley: At the enemy, sir.

Daniel: They weren't human beings?

Calley: Yes, sir.

Daniel: They were human beings?

Calley: Yes, sir.

Daniel: Were they men?

Calley: I don't know, sir, I would imagine they were, sir.

Daniel: Didn't you see?

Calley: Pardon, sir?

Daniel: Did you see them?

Calley: I wasn't discriminating.

Daniel: Did you see women?

Calley: I don't know, sir.

Daniel: What do you mean you weren't discriminating?

Calley: I didn't discriminate between individuals in the village, sir. They were all the enemy, they were all to be destroyed, sir.

Despite concerted public pressure to absolve Calley, a court martial found him guilty. That the military could not condone an indiscriminate slaughter of civilians is evidence that a guilty conscience, or even a sense of moral values, may exist even in extremely violent cultures, such as that cultivated by sections of the US military during the Vietnam war[7]. Moreover, many of the young US soldiers who went to Vietnam returned to join the burgeoning peace movement. The experience of the banality of violence in the charnel-house that was Vietnam was, in many cases, countermanded by reason and hope. We may worry that our moral responses can become dammed-up and walled-in by indifference and fear, but, even in situations in which violence swamps the personality, non-violent options are adopted by many people.

Calley may have lost his capacity for moral judgment, and discarded any vestige of human compassion, but he was neither unique, nor, indeed, particularly unusual: the role call of genocide and terror is depressingly long in human history.

Violent responses seem to exist within a continuum of human reactions rather than as a distinct and separate category. It is not always easy to maintain a non-violent position in the face of the terrors of the world. Take, for example, the 'trial' of the Ceausescus. The West, in the main, applauded when the Romanian army turned its guns and tanks on the supporters of the dictator, Nicolae Ceausescu. If the same weapons, wielded by the same soldiers, had been turned on the Romanian people - even if they were themselves armed - most countries would have cried: 'genocide', 'repression', 'evil'.

---

7   *Although Calley was sentenced to life imprisonment, he was later released on parole.*

Moreover, when the elderly despot and his wife were given a short, trumped-up 'trial' and bloodily executed, nobody wept and most people nodded understandingly. If the dictator had conducted a trial of similar abruptness on two septuagenarians a cry of rage and execration would have rung out around the world. The cultural paradox of violence is that force can never be vindicated, except in those cases in which it can.

In order to interpret the cultural representation of violence, we must understand the shuttle back and forth between the fear of chaos engendered by violence and the need for social order - which is guaranteed ultimately by physical force. At some level, attitudes to violent images on television must relate to our opinions about the type of violence which a society may consider necessary for its own protection.[8]

Signs

The expression of violence in dramas, entertainments, rites and symbols is seldom simple. It is not often easy to assess whether a story, a myth or an event is meant to be taken as a genuine expression of violent acts which people wish to see, or as the fictional, playful, enactment of actions which people devoutly hope will never occur in real life. Research in Britain has revealed consistently that a great many people are concerned that our sensitivities may be poisoned imperceptibly - image by image, story by story - by exposure to violence.

The anthropologist, Clifford Geertz, explored the ambiguity of the theatrical expression of violence in his work on Balinese cockfights.[9] His study may have considerable relevance for our understanding of how audiences come to understand violent acts and stories on television.

The cockfight is, according to Geertz, an event in which the 'creative power of aroused masculinity and destructive power of loosened animality fuse in a bloody drama of hatred, cruelty, violence, and death.' In essence, two fighting cocks with spurs attached to their legs rip each other apart until one dies. The contradiction, in Geertz's eyes, is that the Balinese are 'shy to the point of obsessiveness of open conflict. Oblique, cautious, subdued, controlled, masters of indirection and dissimulation ... they rarely face what they can turn away from, rarely resist what they can evade.' However, in the cockfight the Balinese portray themselves as 'wild and murderous, with manic explosions of instinctual cruelty.'

---

8 *In the BSC's 1989 survey, most respondents expressed a view that violence was always or often acceptable in order to protect one's family, defend the country, prevent cruelty to animals, and to prevent a violent crime. See,* **Broadcasting Standards Council Annual Report 1988-1989,** *page 38.*

9 *Geertz, C. (1973)* **The Interpretation of Cultures,** *Basic Books pp 412-453.*

Geertz explores this apparent cultural paradox by utilising the idea of deep play, culled from the work of the utilitarian philosopher, Jeremy Bentham.[10] Such play occurs when a gambler is in over his head - for example, if he or she has £500 and bets it all on the turn of a card. Cultural deep play occurs in the cockfight because the bets and the fights dramatize and symbolize status conflicts; sociologically, the gamblers are in over their heads. However, the cockfight expresses suppressed tension within the community, it is only an act, an entertainment. Nothing really changes in the village but, for a brief and dramatic moment, the participants take part in a story - the cockfight - which explores what it would be like **if** their personality and their society could be transformed. As Geertz puts it: 'The slaughter in the cock ring is not a depiction of how things literally are among men, but, what is almost worse, of how, from a particular angle, they imaginatively are.'

Television violence, as a product of a mass medium, is profoundly more complicated than the cockfight, but Geertz's analysis of deep play may help us to understand something of our own culture. If we take the other meaning of 'play', as a performance or an entertainment, the metaphor of a deep or shallow play may usefully be applied. In television fiction everything stands for something else; actors are rewarded if we, the audience, can believe - for the duration of the programme - that they have taken on the personality of someone else; writers are applauded if they present to the audience a powerful, intriguing, imaginative world; directors, editors and crew are praised if the images and story are integrated in a coherent or convincing way.

At one level, the creators of violent entertainment are telling us a story about characters and about what the world is, or should be like. However, the stories reveal also what the creators of the drama think of the ability of their audience to understand and to follow the story. Like the cockfight, though, it is difficult to be certain about the message which the audience brings to and takes from the story. Does violent entertainment nervously pick away culturally at our exposed viscera; are Britain's wounds re-opened each day by television programmes? Does television contain any deep play, or is it fundamentally shallow?

Deep play may occur when British viewers feel that a fiction is an indictment on British life, or if a drama contains violence which viewers can see on our streets. Such entertainments may trigger anxious concern about the possible effects of the images or resentment at the inaccurate depiction of British society. However, if the same acts of violence are portrayed in a cartoon, in a Western, in a Hollywood gangster film, or in a Hammer Horror film, this may constitute

---

10 *The phrase is drawn from* **The Theory of Legislation,** *(1931) International Library of Psychology, note to page 106*

shallow play which leaves most people untroubled. Culturally, and socially, there is little or nothing at stake in shallow play.

If deep play has some value as a concept, it should help us to make sense of differences between attitudes to straightforward horror films, such as **A Nightmare on Elm Street** and serious dramas about British life, such as **The Firm**.[11] Moreover, we should be able to see how the meaning of assertions about violence on television are related to our opinions about violence in society. Before turning to television, therefore, the next section explores some difficult questions. Do our habitual ways of thinking about the world include violence? Do we approve of violence? What sort of violence would we accept as an appropriate response to crime?

---

11 **The Firm**, *a play which explored the causes of football hooliganism, was broadcast on BBC2 on the 8th February, 1989.*

3.

Times of Trouble

Decline and fall?

On 2nd January, 1863, **The Times** proclaimed: 'The dangerous classes seem to be getting the better of society ... Under the influence of philanthropic sentiments and a hopeful policy, we have deprived law of its terrors and justice of its arms.' We seem always to look back to an age of peace and of order; a time before the violence seeped in.[12] The present age seems always to be more uncertain and dangerous than the past.

It is difficult to evaluate the relative increase in crime from 1890 to 1990; the number of policemen and method of policing tend to affect the number of crimes which are reported. However, according to recent Home Office figures, violence against the person increased by 12% between 1987 and 1988; most of these offenses were pub brawls, football hooliganism and domestic conflicts. Even this rise is slightly suspect. The increase in reported rapes was affected by new instruction issued to the police to treat rape victims with more care, and, by implication to report rape more carefully. After this guidance had been issued, 50 per cent more rapes were recorded in one London borough alone.[13]

No matter what the reporting effect, it is reasonably clear that between 1978 and 1988 woundings and assaults rose considerably (by 80 per cent according to recent Home Office figures.) However, in assessing the ways in which people perceive this increase in violent crime, it is important to stress that in 1988 violence comprised 6% of all recorded offenses, and that rape, armed robbery and crimes which endangered life made up one-third of one percent of all criminal activities.

---

12 *See Pearson, G. (1983)* **Hooligan: A History of Respectable Fears,** *Macmillan. Humphries, S. (1981)* **Hooligans or Rebels?: An Oral History of Working Class Childhood and Youth 1889-1939,** *Basil Blackwell.* Both books explore the level and nature of street crime in the 19th Century.

13 *See* **Tackling Crime,** *(1989), Home Office, p12.*

Although the figures reveal that most people will seldom, if ever, be subjected to a violent attack, a great many people in Britain **feel** that they live in a violent society. In the current Broadcasting Standards Council survey, on which this report is based, around half of the respondents thought that Britain was a markedly violent place in which to live.[14] Older people (65+) were particularly concerned that Britain was unsafe; almost two in three (62%) who responded to the survey were convinced that Britain was violent.

The idea that Britain is on a slippery slope to an even more cruel culture is deeply embedded in people's minds. Most people in the survey thought that Britain had become more violent (68%) or much more violent (15%) since 1980.[15] Interestingly, young people aged between sixteen and twenty-four were convinced (73%) that they were now living in a more violent country than the one in which they had spent their childhood.

A great many of the reasons for the increase in violence which were offered spontaneously by those who thought that Britain had become more violent, focused on the failure of parents to control or communicate with their children. For example, many of these respondents (19%) worried about the lack of discipline in homes. Examples of parental indifference or inadequacies (11%) were cited among other family-based reasons as the cause of the increase in violence (which made up 22% of the total number of reasons mentioned by respondents as being responsible for the rise.)[16]

Other respondents (11%) thought that the source of the indiscipline lay with a lax education system (5% of total number of reasons). A general collapse of

---

14 *Question: 'Can you tell me how violent you think British society is today?' Not very violent, 11%; quite violent, 41%; violent, 17%; very violent, 23%; extremely violent, 7%; don't know, 1%. N=total sample, 1009. For men the combined score on the last three violence categories was 44%, for women, 49%.*

15 *Question: 'Compared to ten years ago, overall do you think that society has become more or less violent?'*
Much less violent, 0%; less violent, 2%; as violent now as it was then 13%; more violent, 68%; much more violent, 15%; don't know, 2%. N=1009.

16 *There are two ways to calculate these figures. The first is to look at the percentage of respondents who hold the view, the second is to take a percentage of the total number of responses=1965.*

authority and restraint was held to be responsible for the increase by some people (10%); whereas a number felt that Britain's problems were the result of swelling unemployment figures (18% of respondents, or 9% of total number of reasons mentioned) or, simply, poverty (9% of respondents or 5% of reasons).

Not a few people blamed the increase in violence on selfishness (2%), self-centredness (3%) and materialism (9%). Television (17%) and videos (4%) were found culpable by a number of people who were troubled that the representation of violence may have consequences in the real world[17].

Similar responses emerged when respondents were invited to identify the **primary** reason for this upward spiral of violence. Almost half (46%) were convinced that the deep, underlying problem was that most homes lacked discipline. Unemployment was identified as the major cause of violent behaviour by a considerable number of respondents (21%), whereas diminishing numbers felt that the most pressing difficulties for Britain were a lack of discipline in schools (14%) and television (12%). (Other options were: poor or overcrowded housing (4%), a decline in religion (3%), and newspapers (2%).)[18]

If most people are convinced of the violent nature of British life, and many are troubled by the sense of indiscipline which they feel is emblematic of a society not at one with itself, what kind of solutions do they wish to see implemented? Do British people believe that the only sensible response to violence is violence itself?

Fitting the crime

A large majority of respondents who took part in the survey (63%) felt that misdemeanours by boys in school should be met by physical force in the shape

---

17 Question: 'What do you consider to be the reasons for society becoming more violent?' The question was open-ended and respondents who thought that Britain had become more violent (N=836) were allowed to state as many reasons as they wished.

18 Question: 'I would like you to rank these according to how much you consider them to have contributed to increased violence in society. Firstly, can you name which one you think has contributed the most to the increase in violence? And now I'd like you to name the second most influential factor. And the third, etc.' N= all those who think that Britain has become more violent (836). The rank order was the same across ages and socio-economic groups.

In 1988, a similar question about violent crime elicited similar responses: lack of discipline in the home, 41%; unemployment, 24%; television, 10%; lack of discipline in schools, 10%; poor housing, poverty, 5%; break up old communities, 4%; the decline of religion, 3%; other, 2%; don't know, 3%. See Docherty, D. Morrison, D.E. Tracey, M. (1988) **Keeping Faith? Channel 4 and its Audience,** John Libbey.

of the belt or the cane; moreover, just over half of the respondents (51%) thought that such punishments may be administered to girls.[19] Most supporters of corporal punishment were content to see the belt and the cane administered to boys (86%) and girls (84%) aged between ten and fourteen.

Not everyone accepted that physical punishment was an appropriate response to a child's lack of discipline; for example, more women (41%) than men (26%) were unhappy with the idea that teachers should administer the belt or the cane to boys; furthermore, over half of the respondents who were aged between sixteen and twenty-four (55%) predictably came out against such punishment in schools.

Capital punishment for the crime of pre-meditated murder brought forth a mixed response from respondents. Although large numbers of people (44%) supported the death penalty, it was not endorsed overwhelmingly; indeed, the majority opted for some form of jail sentence - such as imprisonment until natural death (35%), life imprisonment for at least twenty years (14%), and imprisonment until the murderer reforms (5%). [20]

(Again, women (38%) were less likely than men (49%) to opt for capital punishment, and people over the age of thirty-five (51%) approved of this type of punishment more than younger people (34%).)

Many of those who sanctioned the death penalty did not wish to see it administered in a particularly brutal manner: half (51%) opted for the injection of a lethal drug. Other options included hanging (28%), the electric chair (10%), gas chamber (3%), shooting (3%), and a variety of other methods (including a couple of people who wanted to replace animal tests with experiments on the convicted murderer or who wanted to subject killers to slow, painful torture.)[21]

Opinion about appropriate punishment for rape was divided also between violent and non-violent options. Castration (43%), forcible sterilisation (19%), the birch (15%), and the death penalty (10%), when taken together, were approved of more than compulsory psychiatric treatment (37%). Women (47%) were rather more likely than men (38%) to demand castration, but apart from this difference, both sexes responded similarly to the question.[22]

---

19 Question: 'On boys (girls) of what age(s) do you think that teachers should be allowed to use the cane or the belt? You may mention as many or as few as you wish.' N=total sample, 1009.

20 Question: 'Which one of the sentences on this card do you consider most appropriate for the crime of murder, where the killing has been planned in advance?' N=total sample, 1009. However, a further question: 'Are there any circumstances in which you would consider capital punishment an appropriate sentence?' elicited a positive answer from another 29% of the total sample.

21 Question: 'Which method of capital punishment would be most appropriate for use in Britain today?' N= all who approved of capital punishment or who subsequently answered 'yes' to the question: 'Are there any circumstances in which you would consider punishment an appropriate sentence?' ,733 .

22 Question: 'Which of these sentences - apart from imprisonment - would you consider appropriate for a man convicted of rape?' N=total sample, 1009.

Arms and the Men

Although most people who took part in the survey felt that they lived in a violent society, and a majority seemed willing to counter violence by subjecting criminals to violent punishments, most people remained ambivalent about arming the police. Few respondents (11%) felt that the police should always carry guns; however, there was considerable support for the argument that certain violent situations require a fully armed force.

Most people (79%) felt that the police should not be armed when they attend large demonstrations - even if the crowd is throwing stones. The same number of people expressed disapproval of an armed police raid on a heroin factory in which it was known in advance that the inhabitants were not armed. However, most people (84%) felt that the police should carry guns when responding to an armed robbery.[23]

When invited to reflect on the type of equipment which a Neighbourhood Watch scheme should be allowed to carry, a small number of people (9%) wished them to carry truncheons, but the majority opted for non-violent solutions such as walkie-talkies[24]. Similarly, when asked if women should legally be allowed to carry weapons to protect themselves, only a small number of women selected a knife (5%), although many more (20%) thought a sharp object was acceptable. Finally, almost half of the female respondents (45%) wanted a gas spray, and the majority thought that an alarm was the most acceptable method (76%).

What story about Britain emerges from these statistics? They do not seem to reveal a nation brutalised and at war with itself; considerable numbers of people rejected corporal or capital punishment, and around half the population (53%) claimed not to be worried that they themselves would physically be attacked. However, these bare, descriptive statistics do uncover a strong sense among many people that there exists in Britain a powerful culture of violence which must be met with a violent response. A large number of British citizens feel that authority is maintained and chaos averted by the belt, cane and gun. How is this fear of violence and sanctioning of force reflected in our attitudes to television?

Through square eyes

If it is true that television is inherently brutalising, the opinions of heavy consumers of programmes, and of satellite television users who buy a new service

---

23 *Question: 'Under which of the following conditions do you think that the police should be allowed to carry guns?' Tick start and rotate options. N=total sample, 1009.*
24 *Question: 'The Neighbourhood Watch scheme involved local householders gathering together to watch each other's houses and trying to prevent local crime. What equipment do you think they should be allowed to carry or have with them?' Multi-coding possible. N=total sample, 1009.*

to extend their choice of television, should offer some clues as to the nature and extent of the power of television to sponsor violence. The US researcher, George Gerbner, has been running studies since 1967 in which he claims that those who watch large amounts of television have a distorted view of the world; they believe that the world is violent and they are afraid as a result. Moreover, Gerbner argues that television has a desensitizing effect on our moral sensibilities.[25]

One almost has a sense from Gerbner's work of viewers cowering behind locked doors, trembling at the chaos on the outside, or else of them watching violent television programmes and pouring out of their doors and windows to help generate the chaos. Much of the work of US researchers is related directly to the US experience both of television and of violence. Although the BSC's surveys cannot refute such a complex and well-researched study, they can shed some further light on the idea that the **attitudes** of people who consume a great deal of television are marked deeply and irrevocably by their exposure to the medium.[26]

In order to make sense of arguments, such as that espoused by Gerbner, one must unpick nervously the strands of class, race, age, sex, experience, tradition and psychological condition from which personalities are spun. It is easy to be misled if one does not focus on the full picture. For example, if one discovers that, say, heavy television viewers who are middle-aged and lower middle class are more likely to be worried about violence than their social counterparts who are light viewers, one might posit a connection. However, it may be that the heavy viewers live on the edges of, or sufficiently close to, housing estates which contain gangs of teenagers. The reason for both the fear of attack and heavy television viewing may be the underlying, and well-founded, belief that the local streets are not entirely safe. A story about the influence of television must, in effect, be a story about the society in which television is based.

If television has a powerful effect on attitudes, it should operate in similar ways on most people who are vulnerable to its influence. The first question is, therefore, do people who express concern about violence watch considerably more television than those who do not?

---

25 *See, for example, Gerbner, G. Gross, L. Signorielli, N. (1986)* **Living with Television: The Dynamics of the Cultivation Process**. *In Bryant, J. and Zillmann, D. (eds) (1986),* **Perspectives on Media Effects**, *pp 17-40. Hillsdale, N J: Lawrence Erlbaum Associates.*
26 *Mallory Wober, Deputy Head of Research at the IBA, is doubtful even that heavy viewing of violent programmes of the type broadcast on British television generates much of an effect on attitudes or, indeed, behaviour. See 'The Extent to Which Viewers Watch Violence-Containing Programmes',* **Current Psychology**, *Vol. 7, No 1 Spring, 1988. For a fuller review of the literature in this area see Cumberbatch, G. Howitt, D. op cit.*

One person in five (18%) in the BSC survey claimed that they were very worried about being physically attacked.[27] Closer inspection revealed that women (26%) were more concerned than men (9%); that people over 65 (27%) were more troubled than their younger counterparts (16%); and that unemployed people (26%) were more frightened than people with a job (12%).

The amount of television which someone watches seems to have little obvious impact on the intensity with which they fear violent attack. Heavy week-day viewers (20%) are by and large not significantly more likely than light week-day viewers (16%) to worry about being assaulted[28]; indeed satellite television viewers, perhaps because they are more likely to be younger and in employment, were slightly less (13%) concerned about an assault than the rest of the population.

Similar results emerged when people expressed a fear about being attacked in their own home.[29] According to Gerbner, people who watch a great deal of television should be considerably more troubled about the possibility of personal attack than those who watch very little. However, this survey reveals that respondents who were concerned by the possibility that their home might be violated (13%) were only a little more likely to be heavy (16%) rather than light viewers (11%).

People who watched a great deal of television were not much more likely to regard Britain as a very violent country (33%) than people who watched very little (25%); moreover, light viewers were no more likely (83%) to believe that Britain has become a more violent country than those with a heavy diet of television programmes (84%). Viewing levels appeared not to affect people's judgement of the reasons for violence - seventeen per cent of respondents among each group thought that the problem of rising violence in Britain was the presence of too much violence on television.[30]

---

27 *Question: 'Using the words on this card, can you tell me how worried you are about being physically attacked?'*
Options: 'Not at all worried 16%; not very worried 37%; quite worried 28%; very worried 18%; don't know 1%.' N=1009.
28 *Definitions: light viewers, two hours or less a day; medium viewers, three to four hours a day; heavy viewers, five hours a day. Unless otherwise stated, all figures given in the report are for viewing Monday to Friday.*
29 *Question: 'And where are you most worried that you might be attacked?' Options: 'In my home 13%; in the street where I live 5%; in my neighbourhood 9%; elsewhere in my town or city 51%; other 13%; don't know 6%; not stated 5%.' N=total sample, 1009.*
30 *When the figures were broken down by age, class, and television viewing, the only obvious pattern which emerged was that heavy television viewing seemed to affect the attitudes of middle class viewers over the age of 44. There were consistent differences between heavy and light viewers among this age and class group. However, the figures are too small to be reliable.*

Other indicators of attitudes to violence revealed that respondents who watched an above average amount of television were slightly less likely to believe that the police should be armed, were no more inclined to support corporal or capital punishment, to suggest that hanging is the most appropriate method of dispatching murderers, or to argue for castration of rapists.

The problem for the Gerbner thesis in Britain is that around half (48%) of the people in the survey who were classified as working class and as heavy television users did not feel that Britain was a particularly violent place in which to live; moreover, over half (53%) were unconcerned by the possibility that they might physically be attacked. [31]

People with square eyes seemed not to see the world through red-tinted glasses: they were no more fearful than their counterparts who spent their evenings reading Agatha Christie or Solzhenitsyn. Moreover, heavy viewers were no more inclined to support violence than their fellow citizens who watched very little television. However, although it was difficult to see how attitudes to television were the product of, or contribute to, attitudes to violence as such, viewers did have complex and challenging views about violence on television. It is to these opinions that we now turn.

---

[31] Question: 'Can you tell me how violent you think British society is today? Not very violent, 9%; quite violent, 39%; violent, 15%; very violent, 25%; extremely violent, 12%; other, 0%; don't know, 1%'. N=Heavy C2DE viewers, 195.
'Using the words on this card, can you tell me how worried you are about being physically attacked?' Not at all worried, 16%; not very worried, 37%; quite worried, 25%; very worried, 21%; don't know, 1%.

4.

The Deep and the Shallow

Looking out for more than Number One

In Hamlet, Polonius angrily chides Ophelia: 'You speak like a green girl, Unsifted in such perilous circumstance.' Polonius may not be the finest model of parental concern, but the idea that children are 'green', and that they must be formed and shaped in part by advice from their parents is pertinent to our understanding of how viewers reflect on the ways in which violence may be portrayed on television.

A central theme in discussions carried out among viewers on behalf of the Broadcasting Standards Council early in 1989, is that there should exist an agreement or a bargain between broadcasters and their audiences.[32] The deal is struck, many people argue, between reasonable viewers and responsible programme-makers. When the terms and conditions of the bargain are observed, most viewers and listeners are comfortable with the results; however, if the provisions are broken - by either side - a sense of anger and resentment may develop.

Despite the lack of an actual piece of paper, the idea of a contract between audiences and broadcasters is highly suggestive. There are formal contracts in television. The BBC's Charter and Licence is, in effect, a contract between the Crown (or the State) and the BBC, such that the latter is called upon to perform certain services. Moreover, the independent television, radio stations and cable services have franchises or contracts with the regulatory authorities - the IBA, and the Cable Authority.

The formal contracts do not capture fully the idea of the informal deal envisaged by the people in the discussion groups. Perhaps a more appropriate term to describe what viewers and listeners have in mind is the idea of a pact - a transaction between two parties which is not legally enforceable and which relies on the honesty or simple prudence of both partners to achieve its effect.

The compact established between audiences and broadcasters is necessarily fluid: values change; propriety sanctions different words and gestures; and moral

---

32 See **Broadcasting Standards Council Annual Report 1988-1989**, *page 29.*

systems break down and become less dominant. However, the **idea** of the pact remains despite changes in the terms and conditions.

Viewers and listeners expect broadcasters to deal with them honestly; not to ignore them or patronise them. Broadcasters, for their part, expect viewers to accept that the Watershed is a safeguard and a guide, and envision that parents should take more responsibility for their children's viewing after the Watershed. Underlying the pact is the assumption that broadcasters have a responsibility to viewers' moralities, values, and concerns, and that viewers should allow broadcasters to experiment and to produce challenging programmes. Central to viewers' anxieties is the moral education of children.

Each generation tries to pass on to its successor reservoirs of culture. As part of this educational process, parents and other educators transmit the formal and informal rules of engagement between people. Instructing children to behave according to moral codes is, therefore, a universal concern of every society; whether Bali or Britain.

Marxists may deride moral education as ideology - the transmission of false consciousness - or, in some way, of a mistaken understanding of one's self; however, leaving evaluation to one side for the moment, the universal attempt to transmit values and culture cannot be gainsaid.

Broadcasting, in its present form, is intricately woven into the process whereby moral values are transmitted; like it or not, television and radio cannot be divorced from moral education (although its exact role and importance may be subject to some - probably irresolvable - debate). Indeed, the idea of a broadcasting service which educates and informs, as well as entertains, invites the audience to think of their relationship to television in terms of a social contract. The pact between audiences and broadcasters states that programme-makers have a responsibility to parents - and to the wider society - in the way that they transmit and sanction versions of, or solutions to, moral dilemmas.

In the group discussions last year, one group of middle class women from Nottinghamshire summed up the debate about the pact between broadcasters and parents:

- *One doesn't let a 9-year old child watch some soap operas.*

- *Basically I can only speak for me and my child. If we're talking about children generally, then someone else has to make that decision.*

- *Divorce, abortion, marital breakdown, violence, alcoholism, sex - its all there.*

- *I'd talk to my child about it (divorce, abortion etc.) but I don't want it laced through a television programme over which I have no control.*

- *The problem is the moralising that goes on TV - there's a message in everything you watch these days.*

- You cannot take everything off the TV which is going to be slightly risqué, as a parent it's your duty and your right to control what your children can see and what time they go to bed.

- It would be nice to be able to watch telly without having to think - oh what is it that's on.

The sigh of resignation of the last contributor puts a very human complexion on the pact; some people simply do not want constantly to be weighed down with responsibility. Garrison Keillor captures this emotion in one of his Lake Wobegon stories:

I'm getting tired of being a dad. Love my girls, but I've been a parent long enough. I did what I could. I can't go on being in charge much longer. These kids, this world, are going to continue long after I'm gone, and I should get used to that and even enjoy it. I can't run them.

Violence in drama and entertainment is related firmly to this broadcasting pact, which itself flows from concerns about children and the character of British society. However, as the next section demonstrates, moral education is not considered by most people to involve the cosy transmission of platitudes; rather, most people want children to be exposed to the harsher realities of the modern world - as long as there is an educational value in so doing.

Growing up

Hugh Greene - one of the BBC's most influential Director-Generals - claimed in the 1960s that broadcasters must ask if the 'Emperor has any clothes'. A great many people who took part in the BSC's research in 1989 and 1990 would, within reason, have supported a position similar to that espoused by Greene. As part of television's responsibility to society, it has a duty to expose difficult moral issues - including those which involve death and violence.

Audiences may reject individual works, or regard the justification for violence as specious, but a majority of people support the principle that programme-makers should be allowed to experiment. The broadcasting pact stipulates, however, that broadcasters must exercise proper editorial judgements and, in particular, that the programme must be scheduled sensitively.

One simple point supports this argument: most people who responded to the survey (74%) accepted that television programmes need not always be suitable for children; however, close to half of the people with children aged five or more living with them (42%) claimed to have turned off the television set in the past six months as a result of seeing a programme which was unsuitable for children.[33]

Most people are convinced that young teenagers are capable of seeing and understanding scenes of death, birth, slaughter and pain. For example, when asked about the age at which a child could cope with a number of different documentaries shown in school, most respondents thought that twelve-year-old children could cope with a documentary about the death of Jews in prison camps. The average age at which it seemed suitable for children to watch a programme depicting open-heart surgery, or another about people who had suffered major burns in a fire, was eleven-and-a-half. Finally, a documentary on a baby being born was regarded as a suitable subject for children aged around ten. It is noteworthy, however, that parents of young children were comfortable with children aged around eight-and-a-half watching a film in which a baby was born.[34]

Although many parents and adults were concerned about the moral education of children, and were worried that they may be confronting aspects of the world too young, most feel that children should learn to confront difficult subjects. It is part of moral education to know that the world contains death and suffering, and to know why. However, there has to be a point to the depiction of these events; they have to possess an educational quality. Explanation and understanding must accompany the images.

Entertaining violence

When exploring violence on television, it is too easy to fall into the trap of not representing much of the violence for what it is - namely, entertainment.[35] A custard pie in the face in a Charlie Chaplin film is violence; so is Jerry hammering Tom over the head with an anvil. Likewise, Dracula biting into the neck of a young virgin is violence, and squealing tyres and screaming policemen in a cop show spells violence. If we are to understand deep play and shallow play, we must

---

33 *Questions: 'Do you think that* **all** *television programmes should be suitable for* **children under the age of 16** *to watch regardless of the time of day or evening?' Yes 24%; No 74%; don't know 3%. N=total sample, 1009.*

'Have you switched off the television set, in the last six months, when you were watching with your children, or turned to another channel because you felt that the programme was **unsuitable** *for family viewing and not just because you or they were bored?' Yes 42%; No 46%; not stated 12%. N=parents with children aged five or more living in the home, 323.*

34 *Similar results emerged from questions about fictional films which featured these subjects.*

35 *Huizinga, J. (1949)* **Homo Ludens**, *RKP, remains a consistently stimulating exploration of the role of play in culture. For an interesting argument on the developmental function of play see Harris, P. L. (1989)* **Children and Emotion: The Development of Psychological Understanding**, *Basil Blackwell, pp 51-80.*

move away from purely abstract questions about violence on television and explore the public's perception of the type of fighting, murder or beatings that exist in Agatha Christie novels or Hammer Horror films.

In this survey, we attempted to circumvent the problem of abstracted violence by inviting respondents to play a game similar to the board game, **Cluedo**. Instead of Colonel Mustard killing Miss Scarlet in the library with a lead pipe, we offered the people who took in the survey the following scenario:

We would now like you to imagine you are a television director and that you are developing a television programme.

The story is a crime story about a murder, and we would like you to pick the person who commits the murder, his or her victim, and the method of the killing. For each part of the story, I will ask you to take the card and tick your chosen person or method, and then place the card in an envelope. I will not look while you are choosing the various elements of the story.

The respondents were shown ten photographs: a young child, a disabled woman in a wheelchair, a young black man, a young white man, an elderly white man, an elderly white woman, a young black woman, a young white woman, a middle-aged white woman and a middle-aged black man. No one type of person emerged as the most popular killer or victim: the young white man came top as the villain (22%), followed by the elderly white man (17%), the disabled woman (14%) and the young black man (12%). The young white woman was top of the victims table (20%), followed by the old white man (15%), the disabled woman (14%) and the old white woman (13%).

The people who took part in the survey seemed not to identify strongly with either victim or murderer. Men and women made similar choices: just over half of the men (56%) and a similar number of women (54%) chose male murderers, and almost the same number of women (28%) as men (25%) chose a female villain[36]. Moreover, age did not much affect people's judgements (although, for some reason, people aged over 55 (21%) were more likely to nominate the disabled person as the victim, than people aged under 34 (10%).

The methods by which the killer could dispatch his or her victim included poisoning (nominated by 29%), pushing their quarry off a cliff (17%), running them down in a car (15%). Others opted for strangling the victim (14%), beating them to death (9%), knifing them (8%), shooting their prey (6%) or setting them on fire (1%). The most important issue from the point of view of this research was: how much detail of the murder did these 'directors-for-a day' want to show? The scale was quite simple: 1 meant that the respondent did not wish to show any details, and 7 indicated that the 'director' wanted his or her show to contain many particulars of the foul deed.

---

36 *These are the figures for men and women after the disabled woman and the child had been excluded.*

After the Watershed, more people wanted the murder to be shown in all its gory glory (25% of women and 33% of men marked 6 or 7), than required that the film show little or no detail (13% of men and 16% of women marked 1 or 2). The average score was around 4.5.[37][38] On a more complex level, of those who thought that television contributed to violence in society, one in five (20%) still wanted the murder depicted in their directorial debut to be shown in considerable detail (ie, they marked 6 or 7). Furthermore, people who had previously indicated that all television should be suitable for children, were not particularly sensitive when it came to the **Cluedo** game; two in ten (22%) believed that their murder mystery should be shown in a great deal of detail, and the same proportion thought that there should be few particulars. Finally, many people (26%) who claimed to be very worried that they might physically be attacked wanted their show to contain a great deal of violence.

The story is very different before the Watershed. The average mark on the scale was less than 2.4; the majority (60%) of respondents wanted little or no detail of the murder; and very few people (5%) were prepared to sanction violent images of death. After the Watershed viewers took their lead from directors like Brian De Palma or Sam Peckinpah, before it, they adopted the style of Agatha Christie or **Murder, She Wrote**.[39]

In another attempt to move closer to real television we offered another scenario:

I would like you to imagine that a television director is trying to make a drama about two teenage boys robbing a post-office at gun point. The director wants to make a point about this issue. For each of the following scenarios I am going to read out, I would like you to tell me, using the words on this card, when it could be shown.

(a) No violence takes place but the boys are caught.

(b) The boys take the owner of the post-office hostage and point a gun at his head.

(c) The police capture the boys and point guns at their heads.

(d) One boy punches the owner of the post-office in the face.

(e) A police officer punches one of the boys in the face.

---

37 Question: 'We would now like you to imagine that you are a television director and that you are developing a television programme. The story is a crime story about a murder, and we would like you to pick the person who commits the murder, his or her victim, and the method of the killing.' N=total sample, 1009.

38 Age made something of a difference. Whereas one in ten of people aged between 16 and 24 wanted little or no detail, this increased to two in ten of people aged forty-five and over.

39 Levels of television viewing, age, and the presence of children in the home had little or no influence on people's scores.

(f) A police officer shoots one of the boys.

(g) A boy shoots the post-office owner

Most people (91%) would be happy to show option (a) at any time. However, when violence was involved in the scene, the numbers of people prepared to broadcast it before the Watershed fell, and the number who did not wish the scene to be transmitted **at all** increased dramatically. A minority of people (29%) thought that the scene in which the gun was pointed at the shop-keeper's head could be shown before the Watershed; however, a number of people (14%) were convinced that this scene was beyond the pale. A marked contrast emerged between people of different ages: for example, 30% of people aged over 65 would have cut scene (b) altogether, compared to 5% of people aged between 16 and 34.

Interestingly, respondents were much more concerned about scene (c), in which the police pointed a gun at the heads of the boys. Many people (29%) did not want such a scene to be broadcast, and only a minority (22%) were willing to sanction the transmission of the programme before the Watershed. Older respondents (65+) were deeply troubled about this scene and almost half (47%) did not want to see it included in the programme.

Moving back to the theme of deep play, it is striking that people who approved strongly of capital or corporal punishment were no more inclined to sanction the scene of police violence than those who believed in non-physical methods of punishment. However, many people (22%) who, in their own **Cluedo** programme, opted for a detailed murder did not wish to see a scene such as (c) in someone else's programme. Despite this concern about depicting police violence, many people (31%) were willing to broadcast before the Watershed the scene in which the boy punches the shop-keeper; however, when a policeman punches the boy, support for the scene drops to 21%.

Backing for the story dropped even more dramatically when people reflected on options (f), in which the police shoot the criminals, and (g), in which a boy shoots the shop-keeper. Scene (f) was rejected by almost four out of ten people (this ranges from 24% of people aged between 16 and 24 to 62% of people aged 65 or more), whereas, considerably fewer people (28%) objected to scene (g).[40]

Even if the film did not have a point to make, most people (64%) and the majority of parents (70%) were content that scenes such as the above could be broadcast in a television drama. Those who objected to the scenes (n=296) spontaneously offered the following reasons: that television had a negative influence on children (41%) or others (14%); that violence was not, and could not be, entertaining (22%); and that the police should not be shown resorting to violent actions (21%). (A number of other reasons, for example, that such pro-

40 Satellite television viewers are, by and large, more tolerant of violence throughout these options.

grammes show people how to accomplish crimes, or encourages anti-social habits - were advanced by small numbers of people.)

People who thought that the scenarios were perfectly acceptable (n=648) also had their reasons. A great many people (49%) felt that it was important for television drama to be realistic; a number (21%) disliked the idea of censorship or felt that the Watershed was adequate protection, and quite a few viewers (21%) simply thought that violence was entertaining and that it would not be much of a story without violent actions. Other people (8%) noted that they would not be affected by the scenes or (6%) that it was important to know what was happening in the world.

Deep In Belfast

In Northern Ireland, more than any other part of the United Kingdom, tele-vised violence might be an issue for viewers. Although the people of Northern Ireland may not be more likely than someone in Britain to see an act of violence, there exists in Northern Ireland a distinctive experience of violent actions which are designed to achieve political ends. The BSC commissioned two different studies to explore viewers attitudes to dramatic violence in Northern Ireland: the first, a Northern Ireland-wide survey, and the second, detailed discussions with people in the Belfast area.

There was virtually no difference between the number of respondents who were disgusted by a programme (22%) in Northern Ireland and those who claimed this response in Britain (24%); however, it is of considerable import that not one person in Northern Ireland claimed to have turned off their set because they were 'disgusted' by a violent image, whereas 24% of those who were disgusted in Britain claimed so to have done.

On every index of violence on television which we have developed in this study - excluding the **Cluedo** game, which was not administered - the people in Northern Ireland held roughly the same mixture of views about violence in drama as those on the mainland. Twenty years of the Troubles has not generated a simple response to the representation of violence.

The in-depth discussion in Northern Ireland revealed the complexity of ideas about drama held by viewers in the Province. Imagine: the day of a bombing in Northern Ireland; bodies lie broken and covered with rubble and mortar in a small town twenty miles from Belfast. The news, on the half hour, carries images of friends, policemen and relatives scrabbling in the debris, picking up pieces of clothing, looking for the dead. If you live in Northern Ireland, what do you watch on television to take your mind off the situation? **The Bill, Dempsey and Makepeace, The Sweeney**? According to the people who took part in the groups and discussions in Belfast, people watch anything which contain a bit of drive and energy (and which may constitute shallow play).

People in Northern Ireland are quite clear about the fact that they, too, enjoy 'a bit of excitement, a bit of action.' Dramatic violence was accepted by the people to whom we spoke in Northern Ireland, if it was realistic, if it reflected a 'way of life'; however, if the programme was 'far-fetched', the legitimacy of the violence was questionable.

There is a strong element of deep play in viewers attitudes to dramas about Northern Ireland.

When you see programmes which feature Irish and local people .... it has to feature the Troubles, because that's the way of life going on here.

You can justify violence because you know that they'll come to justice at the end, but if it's a film, then say it's about here, and there's the paramilitary, you might be working with someone or going to work and meeting someone ...you just never know.

*The **Billy** programmes weren't like that, because OK you knew it was going on (violence), but he wasn't part of it, it was just like a lot of people's lives here.*

A special critical venom was reserved for the 'Hollywoodisation' of Northern Ireland - the theft of the country and its political dilemmas for financial gain. One comment may stand for many:

The ones I hate are the ones with Kalishnikovs all over the place - the one with the Yank who'd blown someone up and then came back over to say, sorry. The whole thing was ridiculous.

Northern Ireland has a distinctive history of political violence. However, when reflecting on programmes such as **Miami Vice**, the views of many of the people in the discussions were little different in most respects from those expressed in Britain, as the following experiment with editing videos, which was conducted solely in Britain, demonstrates.

Cutting Out

Abstract notions of what a scene might look like are no substitute for actually watching a programme and making a judgement as to its suitability. Consequently, as part of this overall project, the researchers sent video-tapes to viewers and asked them how they would edit for transmission the programmes and films contained on the video.[41]

The first programme on the tape was an episode of **The Bill**, a bi-weekly programme made by Thames Television which follows the fortunes of policemen and policewomen in a station in London. The episode in question contained a bank raid in which a policeman had a gun pointed at his head, and the conclusion

---

41 *The tape was sent to 250 representative viewers. However, at the time of going to press, 170 had still to return their questionnaires. The interim results were of considerable interest and, therefore, they were included in this report. A fuller study will be issued at a later date.*

of which was the killing of the bank robbers by police marksmen. Of the 79 people who watched the programme, only three people wanted to edit it, and a further three did not want it shown at all. Clearly, the abstract scenarios outlined in the public opinion poll can be translated into drama without causing the majority of people to be upset or troubled.

The second item on the tape was a BBC2 drama called **The Firm**. This powerful film about football violence was directed by Alan Clarke and possessed a critically acclaimed performance by Gary Oldman. It gave little quarter: it contained scenes in which a young Black boy has his face slashed with a knife, another in which an infant boy puts a Stanley knife in his mouth, and others in which various violent gang fights are depicted. Not surprisingly, such scenes excited considerable comment from viewers; indeed, several people returned their tapes and simply refused to watch after the first few minutes.

Of the 54 people aged 35 or more who watched **The Firm**, thirty-one thought that it simply should not be transmitted; however, fourteen claimed that the programme did not require any editing and that it should be broadcast in its entirety. Twelve of the twenty-four younger people who watched **The Firm** were adamant that the programme should have been transmitted without any cuts, and eight believed that the programme should not have been transmitted. Those thirteen viewers who wished to make cuts before agreeing that the film could be broadcast, concentrated on one or two key edits - in particular the slashing scene and the gang-fights.

Although there existed considerable ambivalence about the film, a second question elicited a slightly different response. Thirty-seven people agreed with the statement: '**The Firm** is a powerful drama and therefore needed strong images.' The comments about the programme included:

It was a powerful drama, well made, well written and well acted. An intelligent portrayal.

Female, middle class, under 35.

I can't see it working as well if any cuts are made. I can't say I enjoyed all the bad language or the violence, but I understood it was necessary.

Male, white collar worker, over 35.

To edit this film would take away the powerful message it contains.

Male, white collar worker, over 35.

The programme highlights the changed basis of soccer violence, from the casual soccer thugs involved in terrace and after-match violence to an organised gang-type of culture to whom the game is only an excuse. People should be aware of these changes and this form of drama/documentary style format receives wider viewing than pure documentary.

Male, skilled working class, under 35.

Comments from the people who thought that the programme was not suitable for broadcasting on television included:

Impossible to understand why this was ever made. Pretty sick view of human society and likely to encourage sicker elements of society. Cannot imagine any one with an atom of intelligence watching this garbage.

Female, white collar worker, over 35.

Television should have a more responsible attitude to the general public by not inciting the sort of feelings that this programme does.

Female, skilled working class, over 35.

*To me, **The Firm** glorifies this sort of violence and may therefore encourage people to get involved in such activities. It portrays the characters as real hard men. It encourages violence.*

Male, middle class, over 35.

I disliked it a lot because I am anti-violence and with today's trends, this film portrays hooligans as heroes. If I had seen this film at a cinema I would have walked out half way through.

Male, unskilled working class, over 35.

I disliked everything about it. I think it encourages every thing we want stamped out in this country and it helps to glorify mindless violence to those so inclined.

Female, unskilled working class, over 35.

I didn't enjoy this .. the scene where the baby got the Stanley knife in his mouth was horrific and made me physically ill.

Female, unskilled working class, over 35.

The final item on the tape was Wes Craven's 1984 cult horror film - **A Nightmare on Elm Street**. This film has spawned a series of sequels and the main character, Freddy, made his television debut in a series entitled **Freddy's Nightmares** - now shown on Sky Movies. The film's thesis - if that is the right word - is that a frightening character with a Trilby hat, a green and red striped jersey and large metal fingernails can inhabit the dreams of teenagers and bring about spectacularly gory deaths. The special effects, which include a bed turning suddenly into a geyser of blood, edge the film close to, and on occasion into, parody.

Of the 52 people aged over 35 who watched the film, 13 thought that it could not be edited to make it suitable for broadcasting; however, 31 thought that it would be fine in its entirety if shown after nine o'clock. Sixteen of the twenty-four younger people who watched the programme thought that it was unnecessary to edit the film, and five thought that it could not be transmitted. The thirteen people who wished to cut the film, took exception to the killing sequences - in particular the first gruesome death.

The people who thought that **A Nightmare on Elm Street** should be broadcast commented:

The only reason I wouldn't want it on television is so that children couldn't see it. However, I've asked all the children at the school I teach at, and most of them have seen it anyway on video.

Female, middle class, under 35.

I thought it was a bit far-fetched, but my 14-year old son enjoyed it.

Female, unskilled working class, over 35.

The film in my point of view is perfect and so does not need editing.

Female, skilled working class, under 35.

It doesn't need editing because it's a good horror movie with good special effects. Plus I like the thrill of being scared to death.

Male, unskilled working class, over 35.

As an adult, I like to see adult films such as a horror film ... if you don't like horror you just turn the set off.

Male, unskilled working class, over 35.

Because it was so over the top it was almost funny. The suspense was good and the idea that dreams could be real was intriguing.

Female, middle class, under 35.

Do you have a **Nightmare on Elm Street part 2***? When you send the next video, could you have* **Nightmare on Elm Street II** *recorded on it with other films?*

Female, middle class, under 35.

Negative comments from the thirty-three people who disliked the film included:

Too much violence, far fetched, too bloody. It made me ill. I could not watch most of it. I hated the whole thing.

Female, unskilled working class, over 35.

I cannot help much with this questionnaire because I found the film so repulsive that I could not watch more than about half-an-hour.

Female, skilled working class, over 35.

I found it violent, disgusting and repulsive. The acting was appalling.

Female, middle class, over 35.

Because of the possibility of young people seeing the video, I feel that it is only right to edit the scenes where bad language and repulsive scary happenings were taking place which could have an effect on young minds. (This person asked for 48 cuts to be made in the film).

Female, middle class, under 35.

The deep play, shallow play distinction may offer insight into these comments. **A Nightmare on Elm Street** contains more violent actions and a great deal more blood than **The Firm**, but these comments show that there is an element of shallow play about **A Nightmare on Elm Street**. The film does not impinge on British life; it was, as one of the 'editors' commented, 'over-the-top'. Horror films which are over-the-top culturally and, perhaps, psychologically, do not raise social or political issues which are of any importance for British people; therefore, there is very little at stake in the violence. The comments from the 'editors' demonstrate that **A Nightmare on Elm Street** was rejected more because of squeamishness than any thing else.

On the other hand, **The Firm** constituted deep play. The story was about British life, British teenagers, and a very British preoccupation with football hooliganism; it explored a type of corruption buried deep in the culture of the people who were watching. To approve of the play, for many people, was to approve of the actions - despite the play's more or less explicit rejection of the violence which it examined. People who were committed to the play explained their pleasure not in terms of the drama, but in terms of its import - its contribution to understanding and therefore resolving a major social problem.

Making Choices

The million dollar question in this research, in a sense, is: 'what do people want done about violent programmes?' They may be disgusted, fed-up, sickened, or appalled by a violent image: they may believe that television causes violence, but do they wish films which contain violent pictures to be banned?

In order to gain some insight into this question, we first must know whether viewers enjoy programmes which contain violence. The people who took part in the survey were offered a list of subjects which films might cover - such as Vietnam, modern horror films, and the Mafia films[42] - which, it was reasonable to assume, would include violent images.

The majority of people (90%) indicated that they enjoyed at least one type of violent film - although, of course, there is a great difference between enjoying, say, **The Dam Busters** and taking pleasure in **Rambo**. However, regardless of the

---

42 *The full list was: Vietnam film, modern horror film, comedy film, Mafia film, thriller, historical drama, war movie, Hammer Horror film, musical. The list was rotated.*

type of film which people claimed to enjoy, the question which followed was crucial. 'Would you give up the right to watch (name favourite type of violent film) if it was widely believed that type of film caused some people to be violent?'[43] Around half (52%) of the people who responded to the survey were prepared to give up their rights in favour of a wider sense of responsibility; however, many people (37%) believed that their right to choose was more important than concerns about violence.[44]

People with access to satellite television were even more disinclined to give up their rights. Most (46%) replied, no, and a number (8%) claimed that they did not believe that films made people violent. Perhaps the most interesting result, however, was that women (59%) were more inclined to give up their rights to choice than men (45%). Choice is clearly more negotiable for some groups in society than others.

---

43 *35% of respondents indicated they would give up the right to watch a well-liked programme (which was named in the question) if it deeply offended other people.*
44 *When respondents spontaneously stated in response to this question that they did not believe that films made people violent, this was marked by the interviewer. Only 5% expressed this opinion.*

5.

Conclusions and Speculations

One of the most important contributions which social research can offer in a debate, is to provide a foundation for the development of better questions. Research should open up debate for further reflection, speculation and argument, rather than put a full stop after an issue. This report closes therefore with a conclusion about public opinion and broadcasting standards, and a speculation about the cultural and human defences which are erected against the influence of the media.

The conclusion is that the key ideas with which to understand public attitudes to violence on television are: deep play, shallow play, contracts, deals, give and take, worry, balancing acts, contexts and stories. The majority of people who took part in this study were looking to broadcasters to exercise vigilance about violent images, without engaging in excessive and heavy-handed censorship.

It is clear - if the survey results can be generalized - that no uniform attitude to violent images exists in the UK. Even in Northern Ireland, with all its distinctive experiences, some viewers despised real-life violence but enjoyed greatly fictional violence.

In Britain, the research revealed that many viewers who were committed to methods of violent punishment disliked intensely the representation of such discipline on television. Other respondents vehemently opposed violent punishments but were content to see them appear in a television fiction. Moreover, many people were deeply concerned that they may be attacked in their homes, but clearly enjoyed war films, or horror movies; others felt secure and safe but hated violent films.

The idea of deep play and shallow play has shed some light on the complex ways in which the importance of violence in drama is assessed. This distinction is grounded in the idea of an audience capable of reading and understanding its own culture, and, whatever else these results tell us, they demonstrate that television does not create its own psychological backyard. Consequently, one must speculate about the strong cultural fortifications with which even the most monopolistic of broadcasters would have to contend if it was to transform the values of the nation, or turn a culture towards violence.

Take, for example, Romania. The question we must ask ourselves about the revolution and the media is not whether television contributed to the development of the mass movement, but why forty years of propaganda and indoctrination failed. Ceausescu presumably thought that television was an important part of his oppressive cultural machinery. However, the people of Romania had other models on which to draw; religion, tradition, hope, and wider social changes conspired to nullify the effects of a monopolistic media (although the events of June 1990 must force us to be cautious in our interpretation of events in Romania).

Whatever the validity of these conjectures and conclusions, it is hard to resist the argument that television will never have its own way in shaping a culture. End of speculation, beginning of questions.

Researchers who worked on these projects:

Julian Bond joined Research International in 1982 after graduating in Mathematics from Cambridge University. In 1984 he joined RI's technical development section, dealing with utilisation of computer modelling and advanced statistical analysis in Market Research. He is the author of several papers on statistical analysis, and is currently Deputy Managing Director responsible for Product and Communication research within Research International.

David Docherty is Research Director at the Broadcasting Standards Council. He gained his first Degree in Sociology from the University of Strathclyde and a Doctorate in Sociology from the London School of Economics. Before joining the BSC he was Research Fellow at the Broadcasting Research Unit. He is the author of three books **'The Last Picture Show? Britain's Changing Film Audience'**, **'Keeping Faith? Channel Four and its Audience' and 'Running the Show - 21 Years of London Weekend Television'**.

Adrian Gonzalez gained a diploma in Management from the School of Business Administration in Sydney, Australia. He began his career at Wreckair Limited and moved to MRA Research in 1985. He joined Network in 1988, and is now Associate Director.

Jackie Greig graduated from Stirling University with a B.A. (Hons) in Business Studies and French. She joined Market Power Limited, an ad hoc market research company in 1989. Now at Network Research, she has responsibility for the day-to-day running of the BSC's monitoring panel. She is a full member of the Market Research Society.

Alison Lyon graduated from the University of Strathclyde in 1980 and completed a Doctorate on the Sociology of Education at the University of Leicester in 1984. From 1983 until 1986 she was a researcher at the University of Strathclyde where she helped to conduct a major study of educationally disadvantaged children. Since 1986 she has worked as a qualitative researcher specialising in media and social research. She joined Fusion Research and Consultancy in January 1989 and moved to Network, where she is currently running a qualitative unit, in 1990.

Jo McIlvenna graduated in 1988 from Christ's College, Cambridge and joined Research International as a graduate trainee. For the past two years, she has been a Research Executive specialising in Advertising and Media.

David Morrison is Head of Media at Research International. He gained his first Degree in Sociology from the University of Hull and a Doctorate in Mass Communication Research from the University of Leicester. He is the author of six books on the media, including **Journalists at War** and **The Dynamics of News Reporting During the Falklands Conflict**, and he has been published widely in journals and periodicals.

Eamonn Santry began his career within Unilever as a marketing trainee. Following a spell in recruitment advertising, he joined Audience Selection, a subsidiary of AGB Research plc, as Sales Manager, and subsequently became a Director. After three years, he left the company to run Telephone Research Limited, a subsidiary of AIDCOM (now Addison plc). He became Marketing Director, when AIDCOM's research interests were restructured to form one company, MaS. In October 1987, he left MaS to set up Network Research. He is a full member of the Market Research Society and sits on their governing Council.

Appendix One

The survey was based on a nationally representative sample of 1,009 respondents throughout Great Britain, conducted within a randomly drawn sub-set of 80 Enumeration Districts. Within these Districts, interlocked quotas were placed on age, sex, socio-economic grade and working status to ensure a fully representative national sample. Quotas were placed according to recent data from the National Readership Survey and BARB.

The questionnaire was also administered to a quota sample of 50 Asians and 50 Afro-Caribbeans. A further 112 interviews were carried out amongst respondents who had access to satellite television in their own homes and regularly watched programmes broadcast by satellite; quotas were placed on this sample to reflect the satellite owning and renting population. Interviews within these three groups were spread nationally.

The questionnaire, slightly adapted to take into consideration the different circumstances, was also administered to 157 respondents in Northern Ireland. Interlocked quotas were set to reflect the Northern Irish population in terms of age, sex, socio-economic grade and working status.

Appendix Two

Fusion Research and Consultancy was asked by the BSC to conduct a qualitative research survey of attitudes towards drama, particularly violence in drama, in Northern Ireland.

The aim of the research was to establish the relationship that the audience has with drama, and to examine the specific context of Northern Ireland when looking at drama programmes with an explicitly violent content.

Because of the exploratory nature of the research, it was felt that a series of workshops, separating Catholic and Protestant respondents, but mixing ages and genders, would be appropriate. As the workshops were designed to explore the ways in which people defended their views about violence in drama, it was important to explore the interaction between respondents at different stages in their lives, and between people who held very different opinions. The workshops tried to capture something of the type of arguments about television which occur in households and in work-places.

Four such workshops were held. In order to reflect possible differences between urban and suburban/rural experiences, two workshops were held in Belfast (one Catholic, one Protestant), and two outside of the City. These groups were split by socio-economic grouping (2 ABC1, 2 C2DE).

Two extended group discussions were held with teenagers. The groups were split between Catholic and Protestant, one held outside Belfast, the other in Belfast. Finally, a series of four 'family interviews' was held. Both parents and children were interviewed together for the first part of the group, then separate interviews were held with the parents and the children. Two interviews were held with families with young children (split by Catholic and Protestant), and two interviews were held with families with older children (again split by Catholic and Protestant).

Appendix Three

As part of its wider monitoring responsibilities for the Council, Network Research recruited a panel of 750 television viewers between 19 January and 25 February 1990. The panel was designed to offer a pool of respondents who could regularly be contacted in the event that the BSC required any specific television programme to be monitored. The panel was recruited to be generally representative of the adult population in Great Britain (15 years plus). Recruitment was conducted by telephone, using Network's Computer Assisted Telephone Interviewing System (CATI).

In order to recruit a sub-panel for the video-editing trial, members of the viewer panel were again contacted, between 27 and 29 April, 1990. The panel members were given details of the video study, and asked if they were willing to participate.

A total of 250 respondents were recruited. As with the original panel, respondents were generally representative of the adult population of Great Britain. This time however the minimum age was 18 years. Again all interviews were conducted using CATI.

Before receiving the video, all video panel members were again contacted in order to give them further details. They were told which films would be on the video and their duration. They were also told approximately when they would receive the video and reminded that they would be required to complete a questionnaire for each programme.

The programmes on the video were **The Bill**, **The Firm** and **A Nightmare on Elm Street**. The approximate duration of the video was 3 hours.

THE BROADCASTING STANDARDS COUNCIL

The Broadcasting Standards Council was established on a pre-statutory basis by the Government in May, 1988. The Council's remit concerns the portrayal in television and radio programmes and advertisements of violence, sexual conduct and matters of taste and decency. It has been given five main tasks:

(i) The drawing up of a Code of Practice in consultation with the broadcasting authorities and others; the Broadcasting Bill provides that the Code's contents be reflected by the broadcasters in their own Codes and programme guidelines.

(ii) The monitoring of programmes and subsequent reporting on standards in domestic services or in services reaching this country from elsewhere.

(iii) Research into such matters as the nature and effects on attitudes and behaviour of the portrayal of violence and of sex in programmes and commercials.

(iv) The handling of complaints.

(v) Liaising within Europe with comparable organisations and with the European Community and the Council of Europe on issues of standards in transfrontier broadcasting, including the protection of minors and incitement to hatred on the grounds of race, sex, religion or nationality.

BROADCASTING STANDARDS COUNCIL
5-8 The Sanctuary
London SW1P 3JS

Tel: 071-233-0544
Fax: 071-233-0397